THE BLACK COUNTRY REMEMBERED

ALTON DOUGLAS

DENNIS MOORE

ADDITIONAL RESEARCH BY JO DOUGLAS

© 1996 Alton Douglas, Dennis Moore, Jo Douglas
© 2007 Alton and Jo Douglas. 2nd Impression
ISBN 10: 1-85858-404-3
ISBN 13: 978-1-85858-404-1
First published by Beacon Broadcasting Ltd in 1996
**This edition published by Brewin Books Ltd, Doric House,
56 Alcester Road, Studley, Warwickshire B80 7LG**
Printed at Cromwell Press Limited, Great Britain.

Gigmill Primary School, Stourbridge, have swept the board in brass band competitions.
Here, they celebrate end of term, 12th July 1978.

Front Cover: Manifoldia Ltd., (manufacturing stationers) Bromford Lane, West Bromwich, c 1930.

Title Page: A view of the parish church, from the main Halesowen - Kidderminster road, Halesowen,
19th April 1951.

The Greater Black Country.

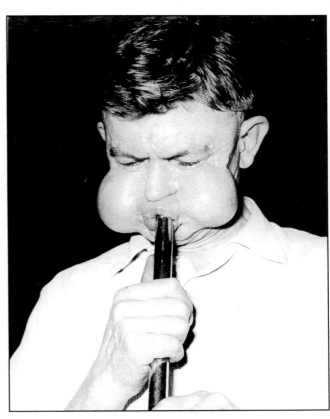

Frank Duce demonstrates the effort involved in glass-blowing, Stuart Crystal, Wordsley, 1970.

Chain blocking shop, Lloyds British Testing Co. Ltd., Proving House, Netherton, 1929.

PARISH OF DARLASTON.

OPENING OF THE
DARLASTON TOWN HALL
AND PUBLIC BUILDINGS.

Wednesday, 31st Oct., 1888.

At a Meeting of the Local Board, held in the Board Room, on the 19th inst., it was unanimously resolved :-

"That the Manufacturers and Shop-keepers "be earnestly requested to close their works "and places of business on the 31st inst., on "the occasion of the opening of the Town "Hall and Public Buildings, and that all the "inhabitants be urged to make that day a "general holiday, and to exhibit Flags and "Bunting from their houses and manufactories."

I venture to express the confident hope, that the Darlaston people, appreciating the social, intellectual and official advantages of the new and splendid Hall and Buildings provided for them, will cheerfully comply with the wishes of the Board.

JAMES SLATER,
CHAIRMAN.

20th October, 1888.

The Stone Cross, Hall Green Road, West Bromwich, c 1895.

High Street, Wordsley, 1896.

The Cedars, Stream Road, Kingswinford, c 1898.

Parkfield Road, Wolverhampton, 1899.

High Street, Smethwick, c 1900.

J. T. Worton's shop (extreme right) High Street, Lye, c 1900.

Visitors to West Park, Wolverhampton, inspect the Monolith, 1902. It consists of a block of Felsite, carried, during the Glacial Epoch, from Arenig, Merionethshire and found in Oak Street in 1881.

Stourbridge Fire Brigade, Rockingham Hall, 1903.

Girls' Society, The Vicarage, Tettenhall, c 1906.

A Black Country blast furnace, 1907.

Office staff, Fellows Bros., Cradley Heath, c 1910.

Commemorating the Coronation of King George V, High Street, Stourbridge, 1911.

West Bromwich Station, 1911.

Queen Square, Wolverhampton, 1912.

Market Place, Wednesbury, c 1912.

Lichfield Street, Wolverhampton, 1913.

9

Walsall Market, 1914.

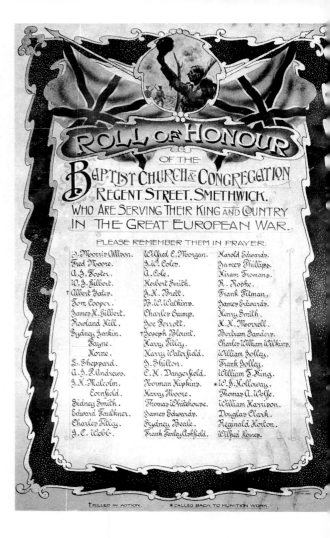

1920

The staff of Bean Cars, Hall Street, Dudley, c 1920.

Hagley Street, Halesowen, 1920.

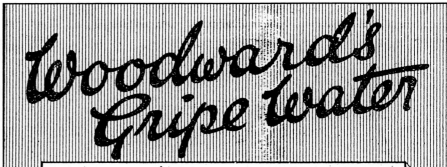
Municipal Secondary School, Newhampton Road, Wolverhampton, 1921.

The Bridge, Walsall, c 1925.

THE WOLVERHAMPTON & STAFFORDSHIRE HOSPITAL.
THE WOLVERHAMPTON & MIDLAND COUNTIES EYE INFIRMARY
THE WOLVERHAMPTON & DISTRICT HOSPITAL FOR WOMEN.

The Wolverhampton
Hospitals' Carnival

Saturday, 3rd July, 1926

OFFICIAL PROGRAMME.   PRICE THREEPENCE.

Testing the bridge, after rebuilding, Spon Lane, Smethwick, 1927.

Toll Gate Buildings, Cape Hill/Windmill Lane, Smethwick,
26th May 1929.

Park Street, from Seymour House, Walsall, 1929.

Standard 7, Bent Street School, Brierley Hill, 1929.

High Street, Smethwick, 1930.

Office Staff, Manifoldia Ltd., Bromford Lane, West Bromwich, c 1930.

Hingley's Bowling Club, Old Hill, 1931.

Clearing up after the floods, Rosefield Road, Smethwick, June 1931.

OUR BAND'S THANKS

The West Bromwich Borough Prize Band wishes
to thank the spectators at the Hawthorns for their
generous support during the season, and trusts
that all have enjoyed the programmes of music
that have been rendered. The band also thanks
Messrs. Dane & Co., Ltd., Messrs. Keith Prowse
& Co., Ltd., and Messrs. Campbell, Connelly & Co.,
Ltd., for providing the music, and the "Albion
News" for publishing the programmes each week.
1931

The opening of the new Hawthorns Station, West Bromwich, 26th December 1931.

Chas. Hales, Heath Town, Wolverhampton, Christmas 1931.

Nicholson (drapers), High Street, Brierley Hill, c 1933.

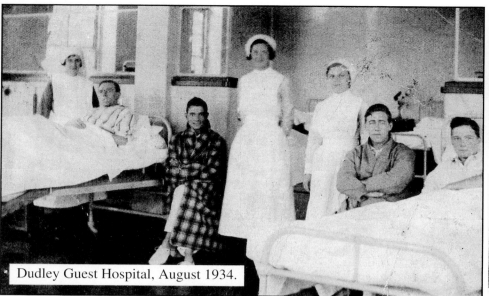

Dudley Guest Hospital, August 1934.

Sandy Powell (centre) principal comedian in the pantomime at the Theatre Royal, Birmingham, looks almost left out of things, as his wife accepts a gift, prior to the opening of the Disabled Men's Handicraft Association Exhibition, Windsor Picture Theatre, Bearwood Road, 31st January 1936.

20

Stourbridge Town Hall, Market Street, 19th November 1936.

Old Level steelworkers, Brierley Hill, c 1936.

Holloware workers, J & P Round, Lye, 1936.

SMETHWICK & OLDBURY ELECTRICITY SUPPLIES

S. W. & S. ELECTRIC POWER Co.

ELECTRICAL EXHIBITION

COMPLIMENTARY
A for Exhibition
period of Exhibition
ADMIT TWO

SMETHWICK BATHS, THIMBLEMILL ROAD, BEARWOOD

APRIL 13th—17th, 1937   DAILY 11 a.m.—9 p.m.

Opening First Day at 3 p.m. by His Worship the Mayor of Smethwick.

ADMISSION 3d.

S.W.S. ELECTRIC POWER COMPANY

Smethwick & Oldbury Electricity Supply

ELECTRICAL EXHIBITION
PROGRAMME

SMETHWICK BATHS, THIMBLEMILL ROAD,
BEARWOOD,

April 13th to April 17th, 1937.

ELECTRICITY YOUR SERVANT

OFFICIAL OPENING.

Tuesday, 13th April, 1937 at 3 p.m.

by

HIS WORSHIP THE MAYOR
COUNCILLOR T. CLYDE McKENZIE, J.P., M.B.

CHAIRMAN—Mr. E. MORGAN, M.I.E.E., M.I.C.E., M.I.Mech.E.
Managing Director, S. W. & S. Electric Power Co.

OPEN TO THE PUBLIC

Tuesday April 13th 3 p.m. to 9.0 p.m.

Wednesday, April 14th to Saturday, April 17th.
11 a.m. to 9.0 p.m.

Ready for the outing, Trinity Road/High Street, West Bromwich, c 1937.

..Old-world charm..in this...
Skippers Sandwich dish
in Spode

WITH STERLING SILVER - PLATED HANDLE AND SERVING FORK.

FREE
FROM YOUR GROCER

It would cost you 6/- to buy this lovely Dish — yet it's FREE ! Specially made for Skippers, in two old English designs, by the manufacturers of Spode ware. To get it you need only 20 Skippers top labels. Begin with the free starting coupon, worth 5 labels, from your grocer's counter. Then save 15 labels from Skippers tins. Take coupon and labels to your grocer and exchange them for the Dish in either of the two designs. Then start collecting for the other design, to make a pair ! But you must hurry, because supplies of the Dish are strictly limited. If your grocer cannot supply the Dish, send coupon and labels, with 9d in stamps for packing and postage, to Angus Watson & Co. Limited, Southall, Middlesex. We'll send you the Dish by return. (*This offer does not apply to the Irish Free State.*)

There's DOUBLE nourishment in Skippers !

Cold weather makes heavy demands on children's reserves of strength. *Extra* nourishment is needed to renew these reserves and build up greater power of resistance. Give them Skippers, Mother ! There's double nourishment in every tin ! The pure olive-oil they're packed in doubles their value — makes Skippers far richer in food value than ordinary fish ! Give your youngsters, and grown-ups, a chance to get safely through the winter. Insist on Skippers, and serve them often !

Skippers
The tasty fish with the DOUBLE nourishment

STAN LAUREL
OLIVER HARDY
WAY OUT WEST

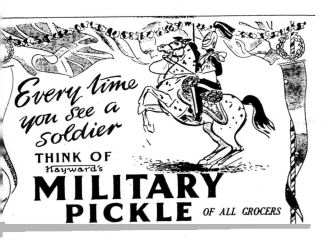

1st Netherton (Hingley) Troop, Baden-Powell Scouts, 1938.

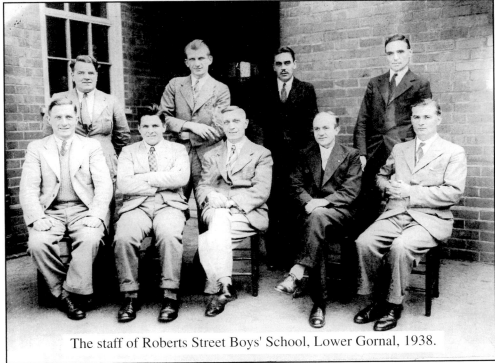

The staff of Roberts Street Boys' School, Lower Gornal, 1938.

Changing a pot, Stuart Crystal Glass Works, Wordsley, Stourbridge, c 1938.
The pot contains the molten glass prior to blowing.

The official opening of the Gala Baths, West Bromwich, 12th April 1938.

A dress rehearsal of "Song of the South" under way, Halesowen Operatic Society, Borough Hall, 18th October 1938.

A tram from Birmingham arrives in Oldbury, 1939.

The Duke of Gloucester and the Mayor of West Bromwich, Councillor Bellingham, visit the Boys' Club in Sams Lane, 29th June 1939.

> " THIS COUNTRY IS NOW AT WAR WITH GERMANY. AS I
> SAID THE OTHER DAY, WE ARE READY."
> After making his dramatic declaration to a tense House of Commons
> yesterday, Mr. Chamberlain went on:—
>
> " Everything that I worked for . . . has crashed in ruins. . .
> " I trust I may live to see the day when Hitlerism has been de-
> stroyed."   4.9.39

The last electric tram from Birmingham to Dudley,
Oldbury Road, Smethwick, 1939.

Alderman, Pat Collins (of fairground fame), Mayor of Walsall, is presented with the Freedom of
the Borough in the Council Chamber, 6th November 1939.

Once again the Midlands were the main objective of enemy air attack at night. One town had its severest raid and its heaviest casualty list of the war, though considering the scale of the onslaught, the casualties were not so numerous as might have been expected.

The raid lasted for about nine hours, and after flares and incendiaries had been dropped to light the way waves of heavy bombers released high explosives over a wide area. Damage was mainly to house property but some small industrial premises also suffered. Public utility services were also affected, but not seriously.

Raids were also directed against other parts of the country; at least five enemy bombers were officially reported destroyed.

R.A.F. bombers chose a single target in Central Germany. They made a powerful attack, lasting about three hours, on the Leuna synthetic oil works, west of Leipzig.

News has reached London from trustworthy sources that one of the results of the R.A.F. raids on Germany has been to reduce the output of Krupp's works at Essen by 50 per cent. The effect on transport is indicated by the fact that it has been impossible to gather harvests, which are rotting in the fields.

22.11.40

The wedding of Bill Reeves and Jenny Moore, Dudley Road, Wolverhampton, 25th March 1940. Bill, a member of the 8th Army Tank Corps., was on leave at the time.

Making aircraft parts. A view of Dept. 19, Rubery Owen & Co. Ltd., Darlaston, 2nd July 1941.

Staff of Wolverhampton Municipal Secondary School, Newhampton Road, 1942.

Officers of the 22nd Battalion Home Guard, Bradmore, 1943.

Home Guard, South Staffordshire Regiment, Carters Green Drill Hall, West Bromwich, 1944.

THE DAY

TO-DAY is VE-Day. At three o'clock this afternoon Mr. Winston Churchill will officially announce the glad tidings that the war in Europe is at an end.

This long-awaited message will close a period of suspense which although it has lasted for only a few hours has seemed almost interminable.

Let us rejoice and be glad that the hour of victory has come at long last. Five and a half years of patience, devotion, courage and hard work have their reward in the complete capitulation of the strongest and most malignant enemy who ever resorted to armed force in impious determination to become the dominating Power of the whole world. *8.5.45*

"CEASE FIRE" ORDER TO ALLIED FORCES

Official Announcement at Midnight

THE UNCONDITIONAL SURRENDER OF JAPAN WAS ANNOUNCED SIMULTANEOUSLY AT MIDNIGHT BY MR. ATTLEE, BROADCASTING FROM 10, DOWNING STREET, BY PRESIDENT TRUMAN IN WASHINGTON, AND BY MOSCOW RADIO. *15.8.45*

The King to Lead his people to-day in Thanksgiving

GREAT BRITAIN WILL TO-DAY GIVE THANKS TO ALMIGHTY GOD FOR THE VICTORY WHICH HAS BEEN WON OVER THE FORCES OF EVIL.

In every town and village, in every church and chapel, the voice of the people of Britain will be lifted in praise and thanksgiving. *13.5.45*

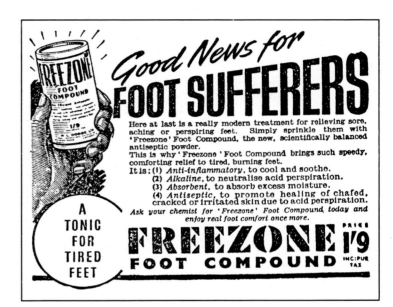

34

Entertainer, "Two-ton" Tessie O'Shea, tries out a bike after opening Kendrick's New Look Cycle Show, Carters Green, West Bromwich, 22nd March 1948.

The first post-war Midland Red double decker buses, bound for the Birmingham-Halesowen-Stourbridge route, 6th May 1948.

Work on the Newtown outfall sewer, Great Bridge,
12th August 1948.

High Street/Rolfe Street, Smethwick, 6th January 1949.

VOCAL AIR-BREAKS FOR WOLVES WEBB

WINNER of the individual award for drummer at last October's MELODY MAKER All-Britain Final, Johnny Webb, drummer - vocalist with the Wolverhampton Rebop Quartet, directed by Arthur Slater, is rapidly making the grade in radio as a vocalist.

His broadcast with the quartet in December last so impressed Midlands producer Philip Garston Jones that Johnny was offered a featured spot with the Vernon Adcock Orchestra in " A Melody Has Been Arranged," and in consequence has again been booked to air with the same orchestra in " Shadows Before " on February 3.

Change of rota at Wolverhampton Baths brings in the outfits of Arthur Slater, Bill Hawthorne and Mac Thomas to feature at this spot.

Newly elected officials of the Wolverhampton branch MU, in addition to president Taylor Frame and secretary Mac Thomas (as previously announced), include vice-president Charlie Cadman and the following committeemen: Jack Clarke. Jack Jones, Rube Rowley, Ron Haynes, Ted Rowley, Johnny Webb and Dave Cadman. 5.2.49

Midlands dealer foils instrument thieves

ON Friday, May 6, at Wednesbury (Staffs) three Walsall men were committed for trial to Staffs Quarter Sessions charged with stealing a complete set of dance band instruments, the property of Jack Bradney and his Band, from Wednesbury Conservative Hall.

It was on the night of April 23 that the instruments were stolen after the usual Saturday night dance at the hall, and on the following Monday morning one of the missing instruments was offered for sale to Messrs. Yardley's, Ltd., of Snow Hill, Birmingham. Recognising the instrument as one sold by the firm two years previously, Joseph Charles Hewitt, the under-manager, communicated with the Birmingham police.

Mr. Hewitt was able to keep the man in conversation until the police arrived along with Jack Bradney, who identified the instrument as his own property.

The suspect was detained, and later the same day his colleagues were arrested and further instruments, including a trumpet, trombone, two saxes, two clarinets and a piano accordion to the total value of £369, were recovered.

The three men concerned will come up for trial on June 14. 1949

Rally hill climb and sprint driver, Ken Wharton,
winner of the British Trials Championship,
Hume Street, Smethwick, 11th October 1949.

The base of an eight-ton hammer arrives in Old
Hill, for delivery to Burton, Delingpole and Co.
Ltd., after a three day journey from
Middlesborough, 1949.

Comedian, Billy Russell, visits St Edmund's School, Dudley, 15th March 1950.

1st Netherton Boy Scouts at camp, Broadway, Worcestershire, 1950.

Albert Hales stands outside Delves Green Cottage, just prior to its demolition, Delves Common, Walsall, 31st March 1950.

Hateley Heath School, West Bromwich, 1950.

Comedy shows seemed to rule the airwaves in the fifties. Here, the cast of "Ray's a Laugh" begin a new series at the peak time of 8.30p.m., with Leslie Perrins, Peter Sellers, Kitty Bluett, Ted Ray, Bob and Alf Pearson and Fred Yule creating the fun and mayhem, 1950.

The stars of the popular radio programme, "Ignorance is Bliss" Harold Berens, Eamonn Andrews, Gladys Hay and Michael Moore, 1950.

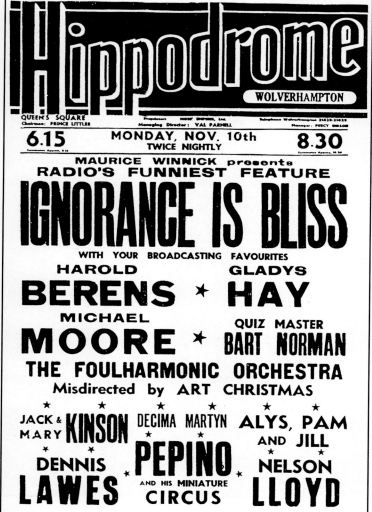

The Square, Oldbury, brightened up for the Festival of Britain, 10th July 1951.

Queen Square, Wolverhampton, c 1952.

'Tis not three weeks *past*, a man called on us for
a *specialle Toole*. He wanted a long
hooke made of *tubes*, *some nine foote*
in *lengthe*, that hath at the end a *Crooke*,
with 3 *tynes* turned *contrarie*, which he
propofed to thruft through open windows
to pull out any *loofe linen*, apparell, or
other *houfehold ftuffes* whatfoeuer, which
hooke collapfeth and is lette out to hooke the
Snappings, which goeth to the *Broker* or the
Bawde, and there they do haue the *readie monie* for it.
He got hyfe *hooke*, and tooke hyfe *hooke*, and to-day
hee did go *Wefte* to *Tyburn*, and we hadde 40 blows
of ye *baftinado* for ye aide we did giue hymme. If fo
be it ye haue any tube *problemme* of this kynde, then by
Bartholomewe Fayre, we pray ye, keep away from us.

*Mr. Accles & Mr. Pollock Metalle Tubes wrought in
diuers fhapes for honeft gentlemen onlie* • • OLDBURY

Opening of the paddling pool, Lawyer's Field, Brierley Hill, July 1952.

Arguably the greatest comedy duo of all time,
Laurel and Hardy, meet Mrs Jones backstage,
Dudley Hippodrome, September 1952.

44

Gladys Road, Bearwood, 19th March 1952.

CHARITY SPORTS GALA

Monmore Green Stadium
Wolverhampton

(By kind permission of the Directors of the Midland Greyhound Racing Co. Ltd.)

IN AID OF
The Wolverhampton & Dudley Institution for the Blind
The Wolverhampton Old Age Pensioners Federation
The R.A.F. Association (Wolverhampton)

MONDAY, JUNE 30th, 1952
at 7 p.m.

Organised by
THE WOLVERHAMPTON CHARITY SPORTS GALA COMMITTEE

Official
Programme
6d.

Danny Kaye, star of many Hollywood films, meets the public prior to his
Civic Hall concert, Wolverhampton, 4th July 1953.

Dudley Zoo at Bank Holiday time, August 1954.

Rescue team from Brierley Hill at Quarry Bank Gala, 4th September 1954.

adio personality, Wilfred Pickles, asks Pauline Dobbie to explain
the rudiments of clothing manufacture,
Hill & Co. (Clothiers), Dudley, c 1953.

Roy Bull, of Brierley Hill, blows "Cook-House" at Trysull Civil
Defence Training Camp, 4th September 1954.

chool children and employees of Marsh & Baxter Ltd., queueing
t the mobile X-Ray Service Unit, Brierley Hill, 9th October 1954.

For Two Weeks commencing MONDAY, DECEMBER 6th, 1954
EVENINGS at 7-15   Matinees : WEDS. and SATS. at 2-30
WILLIAMSON MUSIC LTD. present THE MUSICAL PLAY

SOUTH PACIFIC

As originally produced by RICHARD RODGERS and OSCAR HAMMERSTEIN 2nd
in association with LELAND HAYWARD and JOSHUA LOGAN
Music by RICHARD RODGERS   Lyrics by OSCAR HAMMERSTEIN 2nd
Book by OSCAR HAMMERSTEIN 2nd and JOSHUA LOGAN
Adapted from JAMES A. MICHENER'S Pulitzer prize-winning novel
"Tales of the South Pacific"
Staged by JOSHUA LOGAN   Scenery and lighting by J. MIELZINER
Production reproduced by JEROME WHYTE at Theatre Royal, Drury Lane,
on Thursday, 1st November, 1951
Costumes by Motley   Musical Director : Robert Lowe
Orchestrations by Robert Russell Bennett

Cast in order of their appearance :

Ngana	SHIRLEY EMERY or YVONNE WALTON
Jerome	ALAN SAUNDERS or JOSEPH DARRALL
Henry	ALEKSANDER BROWNE
Ensign Nellie Forbush	PATRICIA HARTLEY
Emile de Beque	NEVIL WHITING
Bloody Mary	HELEN LANDIS
Bloody Mary's Assistant	JUNE PHILLIPS
Stewpot	RICHARD SHAW
Luther Billis	EDDIE LESLIE
Professor	PETER EVANS
Lt. Joseph Cable, U.S.M.C.	ROY LEES
Capt. George Brackett, U.S.N.	ROBERT HENDERSON
Cmdr. William Harbison, U.S.N.	STANLEY BEARD
Yeoman Herbert Quale	JOHN WALTERS
Sgt. Kenneth Johnston	WILLIAM CROFT
Seaman Tom O'Brien	COLIN LEES
Radio Operator B. McCaffrey	BOB MARTIN
Marine Cpl. Hamilton Steeves	CLEMENT HARDMAN
Staff Sgt. Thomas Hassinger	RODNEY MacINTYRE
Pt. Sven Larsen	MARVIN HALL
Pt. Victor Jerome	JOHN VERNON
Seabee Richard West	JAMES ARMSTRONG
Lt. Genevieve Marshall	BRENDA BARKER
Ensign Dinah Murphy	ROSALIE WHITHAM
Ensign Janet McGregor	TERRY HOWARD
Ensign Cora MacRae	MAUREEN GRANT
Ensign Sue Yaegar	VALERIE WALSH
Ensign Lisa Minelli	SHIRLEY TYERS
Ensign Connie Walewska	CAROLE LYN LESLIE
Ensign Pamela Whitmore	CAROLE BRENT
Ensign Bessie Noonan	JANE BOLTON
Liat	CAROLE SOPEL
Marcel (Henry's Assistant)	JACK SOO
Lt. Buz Adams	SEAN CONNERY
M.P. Officer	PETER WHITAKER

THE ACTION OF THE PLAY TAKES PLACE ON TWO ISLANDS IN THE
SOUTH PACIFIC DURING THE RECENT WAR

There is a week's lapse of time between the two Acts

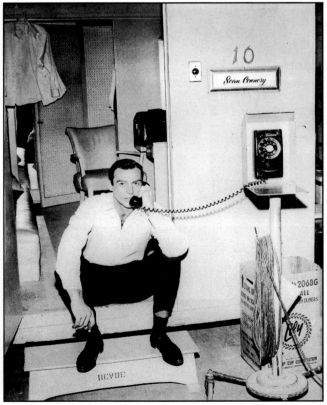

Although Sean Connery is just another name on the
Grand Theatre's "South Pacific" programme, in less
than ten years he had become the definitive James
Bond and moved on to international fame.

Brierley Hill FC vs Stourbridge FC, 13th November 1954.

Church Street/Worcester Street, Wolverhampton, 1955. St John's Church forms the centrepiece.

Hagley Street, Halesowen, c 1955.

Harriers meeting at Wordsley Park, 12th February 1955.

Children's party, Church Street Methodist Church,
Pensnett, 31st December 1955.

Black Country Civil Defence members, attending a coun
council weekend rescue camp, test the cooking at the
emergency field kitchen, Trysull, 25th September 1955.

Hoopla stall, Amblecote Church Garden Party, Stourbridge, 16th July 1955.

A reunion for members of the 11th Staffs. WRAC, Brockmoor, 27th August 1955.

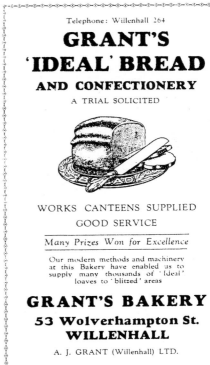

1st Wordsley Troop Scouts receive the gift of a flag from
A.N. Piddock, 21st January 1956.

Staffordshire Fire Brigade (S.E.2) Bilston, with their competition cups, 1956.

A jazz contest, Wordsley Community Centre, 11th February 1956.

Tackle and gear, provided by Fellows Bros. Ltd., Clyde Works, Cradley Heath, facilitate the feeding of cables to HMTS Monarch, 1956. Yes, we wondered too - HMTS stands for Her Majesty's Telephone Ship.

King Edward VI Grammar School, Stourbridge, March 1956.

High Street, Stourbridge, 22nd March 1956.

Dawley Brook Bridge, Moss Grove/Stallings Lane, Kingswinford, 1956.

- and during demolition, 9th April 1956.

ATV cameras today went inside the Windsor Theatre, Bearwood for the first ITV production from a Midlands repertory theatre.

The choice of the play: "Ma's Bit of Brass." 7.1.56

Jack Hawkins (right) breaks off from filming "The Man in the Sky", at Wolverhampton Airport, to knock over four piles of pennies to raise funds for the National Spastic Children's Fund, Queen's Head, Bloxwich, 14th May 1956.

Members of the Sadler's Wells Ballet Company visit Steve & Williams Ltd. (Royal Brierley Crystal) 10th March 195

The Lye stall, St John Ambulance Brigade bazaar, Brierle Hill, 1956.

Inspection of Constabulary, off Mill Street, Brierley Hill, 19th May 1956.

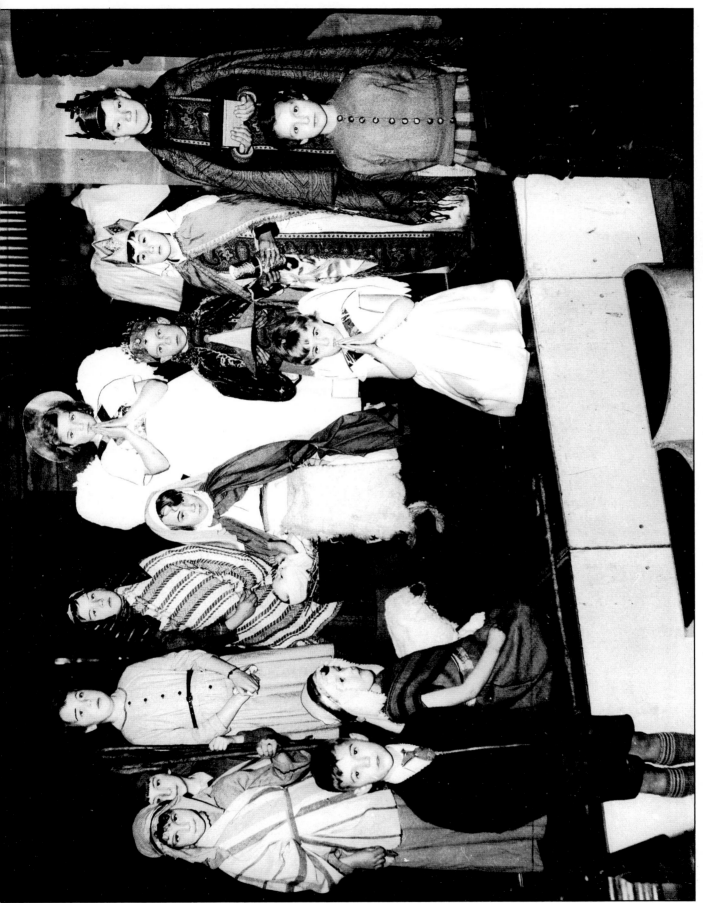

Mount Pleasant Quarry Bank School play, Kinver Parish Church, 15th December 1956.

Brierley Hill Schools' FA Team, 1957.

Queueing for the pantomime, Dudley Hippodrome, 5th January 1957.

Brierley Hill Fire Service Christmas party, 5th January 1957.

...dren from the Sunshine Home, Kingswinford, light sparklers at the Bonfire Party, 10th November 1956.

...Warwickshire cricketers, Eric Hollies (left) and Charles Grove ...meet Colonel Somers (Captain) and T.W. Tivey (Chairman) at ...he opening of the Halesowen Cricket Club's new pavilion, 7th January 1957.

Youth athletics, Kingswinford, 1st June 1957.

WVS members present the gift of a table to Matron, Miss Tuohy, Wordsley Hospital, 13th April 1957.

Pupils of the new Sandwell Secondary Schools, Smethwick, on opening day, 9th September 1957.

The opening of the 10,000th house, Hambletts Estate, Hall Green, West Bromwich, 5th November 1957.

Victoria Street, Wolverhampton, 1957.

Bearded Jack Holloway ("Ralph Bellamy" in "The Archers" radio programme) attends a Harvest Home at The Travellers' Rest, Brierley Hill, 12th October 1957.

Highway Garage, Londonderry Lane, Smethwick, 19th October 1957. Actually, the building had ceased to be a garage in 1938 and was in use as the local ambulance depot.

Dirk Bogarde appearing at
the Stone Cross this week.

DECEMBER 1957

ROYAL SPEECH

BY her Christmas broadcast, the Queen has ended, it is to be hoped, the attacks on the way in which she discharges her Royal office. By her plain speaking, we hope she has also ended the fusillade of criticism which has lately been directed at those very institutions which have done most to make Britain respected.

It has been a vintage year for angry men. They have sneered and snarled away at everything Britain stands for and has ever stood for, without producing a single constructive idea to replace traditions they wish to demolish.

Sneering has become fashionable—perhaps for two reasons. The first is that, like crooning, it is a short-cut to fame.

The second is that we have all become far too tolerant of these Jonahs, far too receptive an audience for the cleverly-aired grievance.

WITTY, colourful and interesting, with a particular appeal for children. That sums up S. H. Newsome's enjoyable "Cinderella" at **Dudley Hippodrome**.

Derek Roy, who was last in pantomime at Dudley three years ago, has a three-star part.

He is an ideal Buttons, a dog lover, as master of Nero, his 12½-stone St. Bernard, and a favourite with the youngsters as a manipulating balloon man.

One catchy song of his makes an immediate hit with the children. They join in the chorus with a deafening fervour.

For Shirley Abicair, 27-year-old Australian singer and zither player, it is her first pantomime. Her style is simplicity—and this makes her a most suitable Cinderella.

She sings with a good voice and sincerity.

The undoubted limelight-stealers are Terry Bartlett and Colin Ross, two enterprising and riotously funny Ugly Sisters.

Their dress can only be described as fantastic. They call on a vast amount of experience—27 years in the same role—to give perfection.

27.12.57

Derek Roy and Nero set out
to collect funds for Dog
Rescue, Dudley, 25th January
1958. The comedian was
appearing in "Cinderella" at
the Hippodrome at the time.

NCB TO TAKE MEMORIAL —OPENCAST

1958

ALTHOUGH it will mean swallowing up a permanent memorial caravan site for retired showmen, the National Coal Board is soon to start opencast operations in Little Bloxwich, Walsall, it was learned today.

The two-acre site in Goscote Lane, with concrete bases and essential amenities for 14 caravans, was provided five years ago by the Showmens' Guild as a memorial to the late Ald. Pat Collins, "King of Showmen".

Town gets 'go ahead' for 30 more houses

5.7.58

OLDBURY'S housing allocation has been increased by 30 dwellings, a little more than 25 per cent states a Ministry letter.

Coun. Alfred Gunn, chairman of the Housing Committee, said today "All the extra allocation, which is for 1958, will meet general housing needs in the town.

"Slum clearance is very important, but we feel we must do something more for these ordinary cases on our waiting list."

Oldbury's original allocation for the year was for 100 houses of which 94 were earmarked for slum clearance families. This left only six for general needs.

The Ministry letter warned however, that the council should not entertain false hopes about the future allocation policy.

"This grant should not be taken as an indication the Minister will be able to agree to any further increase during the year," the letter said.

COUNCIL CHAIRMAN PAYS TRIBUTE

Councillor Horace Partridge, chairman, paid tribute at Darlaston Council to three retiring members.

They were Councillors Gilbert Partridge, a member for 34 years, R. C. Brown and E. Mason.

Wednesbury Hippodrome, 4th September 1958.

The subway under construction, Stourbridge, 30th April 1958.

Whitehall Road junction, West Bromwich, 14th November 1958.

High Street, Walsall Wood, c 1959.

High Street, from the Red Cow, Smethwick, 26th August 1959.

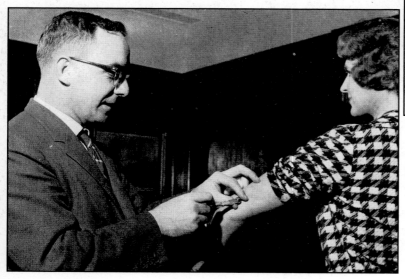

Ouch! Dr Fahy gives Sheila Moore her anti-flu injection at the "Express & Star" offices, Wolverhampton, 1959.

WHEN last night's meeting of the Walsall Education Committee was told that a site had been found for a rifle-shooting range for cadets at the T. P. Riley school, the Vicar of Walsall, the Rev. Vernon S. Nicholls, asked how far the range would be from the staffroom.

"The only answer I can give is that it will be as far away as possible," replied the chairman, Coun. P. Musgrove.

1960

Putting on the style

TEDDY BOYS were still in the news in 1960 and so was rock 'n' roll.

But people were beginning to realise that Teddy Boy uniform and the duck-tailed Presley-type haircut did not necessarily mean that the youngsters concerned were louts or layabouts.

In fact, Teddy Boy garb was becoming respectable in many quarters as these juke-box and dance-hall pictures show.

Nevertheless narrow trousers, long jackets, sideboards and the rest, were still banned in some clubs, pubs and youth halls.

A vertical bender used in the manufacture of alloy steel bars, The Bronx Engineering Co. Ltd., Lye, c 1960.

Taken from the Town Hall tower, the High Street is seen after a moderate snowfall, West Bromwich, 1960.

Walsall's Critics 7/5/60 Answered

Critics of the action of Walsall Football Club in transferring Billingham and Jones, two of their most promising young players, to West Bromwich Albion, were answered by the club chairman. Coun. E. Thomas, when the Fourth Division champions were entertained to a sherry party by the Mayor of Walsall. Coun. Mrs. D. M. Middleton, at Walsall Town Hall yesterday.

Coun. Thomas said that though Walsall were poor financially they would never stand in the way of a young player wishing to better himself and get into top flight football.

Piercy Street/Wood Lane, West Bromwich, c 1961.

Tom Winsper, (left) on his retirement, receives a clock and a chair from K.J. Davis, the Co-Director of J.A. Phillips & Co. Ltd. (cycles), Smethwick, 30th September 1961.

he staff of Willenhall Central School, Pinson Road, 1961.

Former England and Wolves captain, Billy Wright, accompanied by his wife, Joy and the other Beverley Sisters, Teddy and Babs, sings "The Happy Wanderer", 5th November 1961. Some of the proceeds of his record, "Billy Wright's Sing Song Just For Kicks", were to be donated to the National Playing Fields' Association.

The staff of Barcroft Girls' School, Albion Road, Willenhall, 1961.

Comedian, Tommy "You Lucky People" Trinder, conducts an auction for charity, Dudley Hippodrome, 11th February 1962.

The first Socialist Mayor of Bilston, John Roberts (second right) becomes the town's third honorary freeman as the current Mayor, Councillor R. Campbell, presents him with his scroll, 4th April 1962.

The Mayor and Mayoress of West Bromwich, Alderman Philip Taylor and Councillor Mrs Marian Taylor, inspect boots, shoes and stockings about to be distributed by the local branch of the Birmingham Mail Christmas Tree Fund, 9th February 1963.

New Street, West Bromwich, February 1963.

Chapel Ash, Wolverhampton, 14th February 1963.

Walsall headmistress to retire

Miss Muriel Carter, headmistress of Queen Mary's High School for Girls, Walsall, since 1946, has given notice to the Governors of her impending retirement.

Miss Carter was born in Birmingham and educated at King Edward's High School and Girton College, Cambridge. She held teaching appointments at Wimbledon, Bradford and Dudley before becoming headmistress of Truro County Grammar School, Cornwall, in 19??.

For many years a Midland representative on the National Executive of the Association of Headmistresses, Miss Carter was also a deacon of Walsall Congregational (Wednesbury Road) Church. 27.3.63

High Street, Smethwick, c 1963.

Birchdale Ambulance Cadet Division, Walsall, are watched by the Judge, Dr. O'Leary, as they take part in the Walsall and District St John Ambulance Brigade annual competition, Wednesbury Boys' High School, 17th March 1963.

Pat Phoenix, one of the more enduring stars of "Coronation Street", at the opening of the car wash centre at Highland Road Garages, Dudley, 15th April 1963. She played the part of "Elsie Tanner".

WHEN OUR VANMAN CALLS HE BRINGS FOR YOU THE BENEFIT OF THREE COMPLETE SERVICES . . .

★ **FULLY FINISHED**
A first-class service for those wanting only the best—sheets laundered to perfection, table linen with a superb finish only possible with quality laundering.

★ **ECONOMY WASH**
Ideal for household washing and plainer types of personal articles. Thoroughly processed for immediate use and wear.

★ **KLEENA DRY CLEANING**
Good quality cleaning at an economy charge for soft furnishings, loose covers, blankets, skirts and trousers.

send it to

Wolverhampton Steam Laundry

Launderers and Cleaners
150 SWEETMAN STREET
WOLVERHAMPTON

1963

Telephone 26622 (3 lines)

The Mayoress of Walsall, Mrs R. Talbot, presents a cup to Margaret Wincer of the Upper School, Queen Mary's School, Walsall, 18th July 1963.

The procession to the Church of St John the Evangelist, for the Mayor's Sunday Service, Dudley Wood, 26th May 1963.

The Arboretum, Walsall, 27th August 1963.

A view of Walsall Market from the steps of the Parish Church, April 1964.

Construction work over the railway, Walsall, 9th December 1963.

Annual inspection of the St. John Ambulance Brigade, by the County Commissioner, Lt. Col. C.P. Vaughan, Halesowen Grammar School, 3rd June 1964. Halesowen were the 1964 winners of the Worcestershire county ambulance championship.

Dudley Market, 25th September 1964.

Greensforge Sailing Club, Middle Pool, Pensnett, 1965.

Mucklow Hill, Halesowen, on its way to becoming a dual carriageway, 4th August 1965.

Lady Baden-Powell, Chief Guide, visits guides at Wednesfield, 26th March 1967.

A replica of a late 19th century living room, at the Black Country Exhibition, Dudley Art Gallery, 15th August 1967.

A view from Crosswells Road, Langley Green, looking towards the centre of Oldbury, 25th September 1967.

Queen Square, looking down Dudley Street, Wolverhampton, 19th July 1968.

Wolverhampton town centre, 1968.

Annual Prizegiving, with the presentations to b made by the Mayor of Walsall, Alderman Fred Watkins, Little London County Primary Schoo Willenhall, 24th July 1968.

John (Bill) Harrison of Wolverhampton, proudly displays his MBE which he received from the Queen Mother at Buckingham Palace in recognition of his voluntary work for the Royal British Legion, 12th November 1968.

Barbara Stonehouse draws the first pint for her husband, John Stonehouse (right) MP for the area, at the new Woodland Social Club, Wednesbury, 28th September 1968.

Simon Engineering Ltd., Dudley, produced this 40 foot hydraulic platform, one of a fleet purchased by British European Airways for aircraft de-icing operations, c 1969.

Floodwater turns the line into a canal, Walsall Station, 7th May 1969.

THE largest cash-and-carry warehouse in the Midlands opened at Oldbury, Worcestershire. today, Rustons Trademarket, a £500,000 investment, also brings a new concept to the wholesale trade.

Rustons is controlled by E. Laxon and Co. Ltd., of Coventry. Mr. C. S. Sproat, its development executive, says: "We believe that in total area we now have the largest cash-and-carry in Britain, and definitely the biggest selling area in the Midlands."

At Churchbridge Estate, Park Street, Oldbury, the single-storey open-plan warehouse covers more than 60,000 square feet. The remainder of the 3½-acre site offers parking for 300 vehicles. 5.1.70

Council's show house success

A total of 146 people visited Warley Corporation's show house at 17, John Street, Blackheath, on the day it was opened, it was said at the Council meeting.

The house was bought by the Council and modernised in conjunction with the Department of the Environment to give a practical example of how an old house can be brought up to date with the aid of improvement grants. 24.2.71

The Mayor of Dudley, Alderman J.G. Rowley, visits Kates Hill Primary School, Dudley, 18th February 1971.

Champagne for John Shakespeare, Chairman and Managing Director of Joseph Shakespeare and Co. Ltd., to mark his retirement, Old Hill, 12th November 1971.

Karen Eades takes the role of Queen of Light at a special service at the Salvation Army headquarters, Furnace Parade, Tipton, 11th December 1972.

Tuning-up time for members of the Warley branch of the George Formby Appreciation Society, 4th March 1973

American singing star, Frankie Laine (left) meets long-time fans, John and Doreen Bale, from Rowley Regis, 3rd July 1976. The star, who had hits with such songs as "I Believe" and "Rawhide", has more than 21 gold records to his credit.

Wartime shell found

A wartime anti-aircraft shell has been found on a building site in Myrtle Terrace, Tipton.

The shell has been taken to Dudley police station by Mr. John Ward of Foxyards Road, Tipton. It is being kept surrounded by sandbags until Army experts collect it.

The Wall Heath Gentlemen Songsters rehearse a number for their first long-playing record, 8th October 1974.

Other possibilities to maintain the Company in operation have received detailed consideration over the past three months. Approaches have been made to other Companies with interests in the powder metallurgy field and efforts made to secure Government assistance in restructuring the business in a new ownership context, in the hope that some synergy could be established with on-going operations which, would make such a proposition financially attractive. It has to be reported that these efforts have met with no success.

The Round Oak Steel Works Board, at its meeting on the 14th January 1977, had these considerations before them and regretfully decided that steps must be taken to cease operations at the Shotting Plant and the Powder Plant and to wind up the business currently carried out by Round Oak Steel Powders Limited. The Board acknowledges with gratitude the consistent efforts made by all their employees in the Iron Powders Division in endeavouring to make the business a success.

Detailed discussions will be initiated immediately with representatives of staff and of trades unions to explore how the Company's obligations to its customers can best be satisfied, and to ensure the smoothest possible redeployment of the staff and labour force of Round Oak Steel Powders to suitable jobs within Round Oak Steel Works Limited and/or Tube Investments Limited following the closure of Round Oak Steel Powders Limited in three or four months time.

An excerpt from the notice of closure of Round Oak Steel Powders Ltd., 17th January 1977.

Members of Broomfield School of Dance, Smethwick, 20th October 1977.

85

A rousing "Hello my Darling" greeted comedian, Charlie Drake, from the workforce at SCM Typewriters when he arrived to look around the firm, West Bromwich, 18th January 1977. He poses here before rushing back to prepare for his role in "Jack and the Beanstalk" at the Birmingham Hippodrome.

Aston Villa striker, John Deehan, shows the league cup to fans outside Walsall Parish Church, after the Sportsmen's Service, 29th April 1977.

Directors of Royal Brierley Crystal view special crystal pieces created by their company to commemorate the Jubilee of the Queen's accession. 1977.

Members of Aldridge Ladies Circle make a clean job of Jack Moorhouse's petrol tanker, Chevron Circle Service Station, Kingstanding, 18th September 1977. They were raising funds for the Longmore Special School for handicapped children.

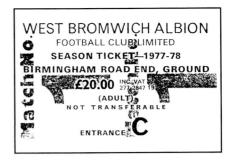
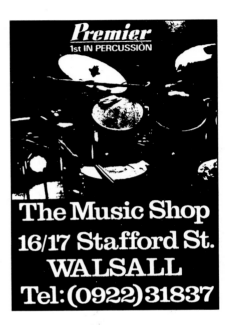

The Sandwell team, winners of the "It's A Knockout" television series, gives a lift to the Mayor, Councillor Cyril Farmer, 24th June 1978.

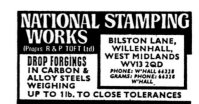

Singer, David Whitfield, signs an autograph for Mike Curry, organiser of the charity concert to raise funds for two of the victims of the Andrew Road shootings. Kingfisher Country Club, Kingswinford, 31st January 1979. Mr Whitfield had an enormous hit with his song "Cara Mia" but was involved in controversy when "Answer Me, Oh My Lord" was banned by the BBC. It was then re-recorded as "Answer Me, Oh My Love".

The starting point of the 3½ mile Sandwell Wedge Bridleway is opened by Council John Ledbetter, Chairman of the West Midlands county planning committee, Wilderness Lane, Aldridge, 26th June 1978. The route passes under the M5 and M and ends up at Tanhouse Avenue, West Bromich.

Father Christmas arrives at the Co-op store, prior to starting work in his grotto, Lichfield Street, Walsall, November 1978.

Walsall's Director of Engineering and Town Planning, Geoff Marsh (centre) acclaims his team of snow shifters as the best in the Midlands, 3rd January 1979.

Youngsters from Hill Top High School, West Bromwich, display their certificates, awarded for proficiency in first aid, 5th April 1979.

Show jumper, Pennwood Forge Mill, with his groom, Valerie
Harthill, visits Alexandra High School, Tipton, 20th December
1979. The horse was stabled at Pennwood, Wolverhampton and had
just retired after a most successful career.

Film star, Diana Dors, meets the shoppers a
the opening of the Sun Valley amusement
arcade, High Street, Blackheath, 22nd
December 1979. She can be seen signing a
copy of her autobiography, "Behind Closed
Dors".

Walsall Market's chief, Len Greenwell, raises his cap to his own retirement, 15th February 1980.

Councillor Dennis Booton, presents trophies to young sportsmen at West Bromwich Boys Club, 7th July 1980.

The Institute of Bankers
Wolverhampton & District Centre

Informal Dinner

TUESDAY, 11th MARCH, 1980

AT THE PARK HALL HOTEL
WOLVEHAMPTON

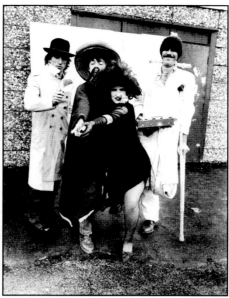

The Oldbury-based Platypus Theatre Company rehearse for their Christmas play "Mrs Frank Einstein and the Missing Bit", 24th November 1980.

Alton, in his role as guest speaker at the annual dinner of the South Staffordshire Federation of Townswomen's Guilds, Aldridge Masonic Hall, 13th February 1981.

Long-serving employees of Dudley Council at an award ceremony to mark their loyalty, The Council House, Dudley, 28th October 1980.

A thank-you to Keith Atkins (left) as he leaves his job as market superviser to take up a similar job in Wolverhampton. High Street, West Bromwich, 25th February 1981.

Terry Thomas (centre), TV presenter of "Angling Today", assists the Mayor of Sandwell, Councillor Syd Pemberton, in launching "Sandwell Junior Passport to Angling", 22nd March 1982.

Jayne Williams, a member of the Halesowen Independent Society, is taken in hand at Halfpenny Green Airport, whilst getting in the mood for the Society's production of "Around the World on Wings of Song", staged at the Civic Hall, Brierley Hill, during the week beginning 21st February 1981.

Drivers of Dudley Council's Charlotte Street depot celebrate their safe driving awards, 10th March 1981.

The Rainbow Man, Gordon Pidgeon, outlines the play, "The Lost Rainbow", to children
visiting the Charlemont Teachers' Centre, West Bromwich, 11th May 1981.

A decanter being blown, Webb Corbett Ltd., Amblecote, 1982.

Guns Village Infants' School Easter Bonnet competition, West Bromwich, 7th April 1982.

The French Flavour comes to West Bromwich. Angela Paskin and R[...] Sergeant provide that authentic look as they publicise the West Bromw[...] Building Society's "Know Your Place" competition, 4th October 198[...] Incidentally, Alton was the quizmaster/writer of the television series [...] Dennis was a member of the winning Wolverhampton team.

The Mayor of Walsall, Councillor Fred Tunley, with a group of teenagers who have gained gold awards in the Duke of Edinburgh scheme, Town Hall, Walsall, 11th January 1983.

Pupils of Sneyd School, Bloxwich, with the Rotary Shield awarded for their school's commitment to charity, 8th June 1982.

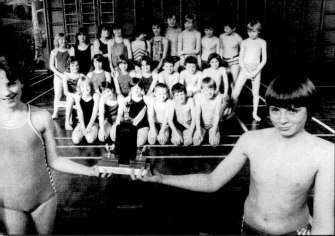

The Manor Way Middle School swimming team, with captains Sara Johnson and Scott Miller, holding the trophy after winning the Halesowen and District Schools' swimming Gala, 8th February 1983.

The view, from the top of a West Midlands Fire Service hydraulic platform, during Dudley Family Fortnight, High Street, 31st May 1983.

Former pupils of Wolverhampton Girls' High School, who left school in 1943, gather for a fortieth anniversary, Summer 1983.

Just some of the children taking part in the annual Dudley Borough Trail, 2nd May 1983.

A fun run, sponsored by the Parents' Association of the Blue Coat Church of England School, The Arboretum, Walsall, 27th March 1983.

Semprini.

Founder member of the Semprini Concert Club, Dorothy Jones, displays the recently-completed tapestry she had made to commemorate the pianist's many recitals in the area. Tipton Road, Woodsetton, 26th January 1984.

Barry Manilow.

Brenda Danks of Dudley (left) puts the finishing touches to her scroll, consisting, of 38,000 birthday wishes, to mark Barry Manilow's big day. 8th June 1984. She was the secretary of his fan club in the area, known as the Sunshine Club.

upils from Wolverhampton's Heath Park High School meet omic, Harry Worth, as he opens the "Write It" exhibition for the ost Office. Moor Street Station, Birmingham, 15th February 984.

articipants in the third Walsall Youth Theatre Festival, ommunity Hall, Foley Road East, Streetly, 21st February 1984.

The Mayor of Walsall, Councillor Stan Ball, prepares to lead firemen through the town's new Fordbrook Tunnel, 21st January 1984.

West Bromwich MP, Betty Boothroyd, with pupils of Willingsworth High School after the annual prize-giving, 8th November 1984. Miss Boothroyd, an ex-Tiller girl, became Speaker of the House of Commons.

The C & A team about to win the tug-of-war shield at Dudley Carnival, 29th May 1985.

Sedgley's Vikki Silvani, helps to promote the seventh Dudley Show, Himley Hall, 2nd August 1985.

Black Country comedienne, Dolly Allen, proves to be the star turn at a charity show to raise money for the Children's Hospital. Crescent Theatre, Birmingham, 10th January 1988.

All the pupils at Annie Lennard Infants' School, The Oval, Smethwick, took part in a sponsored bounce, raising £1,000 for the Birmingham Children's Hospice. The cheque is presented to Miss Isobel Smart, the appeal representative, 20th May 1986.

After a charity fun run, pupils at Aldridge Comprehensive School gather to present cheques to Joyce Smith, head of Oakwo Special School in Walsall Wood, and John Moore, President of Aldridge Rotary Club, for their Polio Plus Campaign. Tyni Lane, 9th July 1998.

Charity events by Walsall's Blue Coat Comprehensive School pupils raise £7,400 for the cystic fibrosis unit at Birmingham's Children's Hospital, 15th July 1988.

Olympic silver medallist, swimmer, Nick Gillingham, starts the cycling marathon for The Blue Coat Church of England Comprehensive School, Birmingham Street, Walsall, in aid of development in the Sudan, 22nd March 1989.

Visitors to Walsall's Leather Museum, 1991.

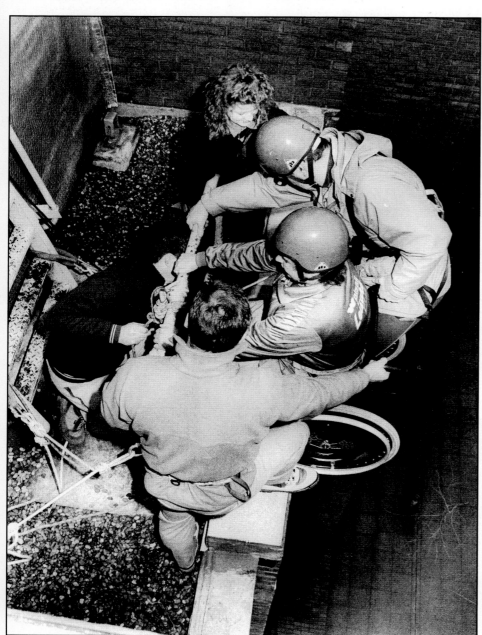

Jean Fellows completes her abseiling trip down the Civic Centre building, Walsall, 17th January 1991.

WOLVERHAMPTON MUNICIPAL GRAMMAR SCHOOL REUNION

THE GOLDTHORN HOTEL
8th June 1991

The Black Country Museum-Tramway

OUT	ADULT	IN
Depot		Village
Colliery	This ticket must be punched in the stage to which the Passenger is entitled to travel and show on demand. Issued subject to Museum Regulations. Travel at risk of Passenger. Not Transferable.	Colliery
Village		Depot
Luggage or Dog		Luggage or Dog

AF 048631

WELCOME TO THE 1992

SANDWELL HISTORIC VEHICLE SHOW

Its Free !!!

Members of the Black Country Tourism Initiative meet at The Manor House, Stone Cross, West Bromwich, June 1993.

Sandwell Park Farm, February 1995. Originally the home farm to the Earl of Dartmouth's estate, it now operates as a late-nineteenth century working farm.

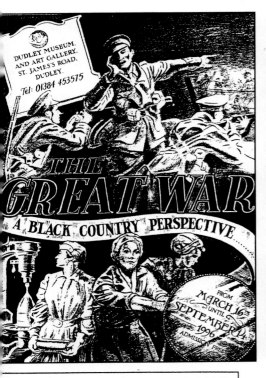

Comedian, Larry Grayson, performs the opening ceremony at Great Bridge Indoor Market, 6th October 1979.

ACKNOWLEDGEMENTS

(for providing photographs, for encouragement and numerous other favours)

Geoff Allen; The Bathroom Village; The Birmingham Post & Mail Ltd.; The Black Country Museum; Books & Bygones; Jim Boulton; Brierley Hill Library; The Bronx Engineering Co. Ltd.; Dave Carpenter; Alan and Brenda Cronshaw; Joe Crump; Archives & Local History Service, Dudley Libraries; Planning and Leisure Dept., Dudley MBC; Rob Evans; Margaret Fellows; Pam George; Geoff Hawkins; José Holmes; Albert and Eileen Hubball; Dave, Thelma and Tom Jones; Kingslea Press Ltd.; John Landon; Eric Leyser; Brian Moore; Sheila Moore; John Murray; Valerie Parry; Mike Payne; Ida Pearson; Arthur Radburn; David Radmore; Royal Brierley Crystal; Dept. of Environment & Development Service, Engineering Services Division, Sandwell MBC; Sandwell Park Farm; Local Studies Dept., Smethwick Library; Horace Smith; Stuart Crystal; Reg Taylor; Dept. of Community Services, Walsall MBC; Wolverhampton Municipal Secondary/Grammar School OPA.

Please forgive any possible omissions. Every effort has been made to include all organisations and individuals involved in the book.

Back Cover: The end of a local landmark, Nagersfield Brickworks, Hawbush, Brierley Hill, May 1951.